MORGAN BOY

BY
NOAH HUMPHREY

Copyright © 2021 by Noah Humphrey

All Rights Reserved

Printed in the United States of America

Cover Art by Anahi Ibarra

Black Minds Publishing is a national publications platform centered around the personal and professional growth of artists and creatives of the Black diaspora. At Black Minds Publishing we aim to give more visibility to raw artistic works, both literary and visual, that center on the healing process of the Black mind, body and spirit. We aren't concerned with the rigid expectations of academia or the "supposed to's" of artistic gatekeepers and instead choose to prioritize genuine works that have meaningful impact for its readers.

Names: Noah Humphrey

Title: Morgan Boy

Description: Philadelphia, PA: Black Minds Publishing [2021]

Identifiers: 978-1-7356122-7-0

Classification:

Words from the Artist

This is for the people of South Central, Los Angeles; this is the reclaiming of our narratives.

We share our stories and lived experiences to highlight the duality of what it means to grow up in a community like ours. Where there is pain, there is also healing; where there are struggles, there is also growth, & for that we say, **"the hood may cry but it also smiles."**

We know what stories they tell about us. We know what people think when they hear our names. The act of counter-storytelling is extremely powerful & that is what we aim to reclaim. People say, "never judge a book by it's cover." We say, **"never judge a hood by its headlines."**

We are powerful. We are brilliant. Beautiful. Resilient.

Making masterpieces out of broken pieces
and let me remind you we are not the ones who are broken, the system is.

We are South Central, Los Angeles.

CONTENTS

PREFACE
It's a Jungle   1
A Still Remembrance; A Dream of Being A Pianist   2
Soil Plus Water   3
The Area I Hold Dear   4

PART 1   5
Smaller Moves   6
We Take Precaution   7
Be Fruitful   8
Wild Thoughts   9
Let's Play Contain the Heart!!!   10
Faces   11
Pressure Within My Rainforest   12
Soap   13
Wanda Coleman,   14
the Great Poet and   14
Unofficial Laureate of   14
Los Angeles (1946-2013)   14
Right This Minute! (Inspired by Wanda Coleman's poem   14
PERHAPS BY THEN)   14
I'll Give You Raw Roses: A Resonating Message   15
Cold World High   17
All In   18
Hood Pie   19
Sumn' Like Black Panther   21
Goodbye To Normal Days   22
Your Own Heroic Survival   23
My Eyes Were On Philadelphia   24

PART 2   25
And You Hated Me   26
South Central Dreamer: A Narrative Inspired By A Jefferson HS Alumni   27
LLD (Our Dreams Have Angels): Rest In Peace Davon "Rico" Spillers 29
 Commandments of Ross Snyder Park   31
I Fought Divide   32
Slauson Elegy: Homage to the Martyr of South Central   33
Dealer of Hooper Avenue   35
The Standing Memories of A Watt's Native   36
The Light in the Classroom   38
One Shot Will Heal You   40
Healthy Homes   41
Negro Memories Are Available   42
Heartaches   43

Wishful Astronaut   44
Eastside Be With Me   45
Resolve Yourself 46
What's In store? A Story of Romeo Doubs   47
On the Daily: A Reflection Inspired By Jarmaine Doubs   49
Move Buildings, Move People   51
"Alcohol is Law"   52
Never Ready   53
Undelivered by the Church   54
The Sun Rises East   55
Picket Fences   56
Acknowledgements   57
South Central Tribue   58
A Moment of Thanks   59
To my Editors,   60
About the Author 62

PREFACE

It's a Jungle

5th grade was rambunctious, rowdy, animalistic, its own jungle.
Each beast went up the monkey bars, all had separate tribes to migrate to.
Some went to forage for food (some didn't share with the rest).
Some went near the shade to drink sweet nectar from fruits;
others drank near the water deposits (the jungle was a humid place). I must
have been a different beast. I tried to fit with exhaustive efforts, but I was
different; the beasts told me so.

I couldn't adapt to the unruly jungle,
and the jungle couldn't adapt to my needs.
I had little communication, no tribe,
The monkey bars were way too tall for me to reach.
I constantly drank from water deposits,
and my mane was ravaged with thick bushy wool,
like a hornet's nests, with thickets of black seamless threads.
I was treated like I had jungle fever,
isolated, non-adaptive, and displaying a coal black mane.

Their hides looked like the day, mine looked like the night.
My camouflage made them attack me, intimidate me, and break my peace.
They mistook my kindness for fangs and my cries as vicious roars
brittled my paths to others and eliminated my places of comfort.
I was alone, hunted alone, and lived far away from the jungle at times.
The classroom was a jungle, the playground was a jungle,
until night comes to the jungle and the beasts would leave
'til morning when once more I would be the same, isolated, coal beast.

A Still Remembrance; A Dream of Being A Pianist

Once a week I used to take piano lessons at the whimsical home
of my teacher, Mrs. Cates,
a lady whose ghostly fingers were stuck to the piano keys
like an eternity.

As she taught me to play, I felt the mastery from her soul--
I sometimes played pianissimo.
My teacher had her forte-esque passion crash my lackadaisical style.

Her crashing sound was stronger, her frail body didn't match her soul.
I saw her soul blazing and the keys of her life had a mesmerizing tempo;
Although taught multiple times, I struggled to know my own notes.

"Patience," she said. She knew my notes would come soon.
As soon as the keys played, I forgot time, leaving my dad waiting outside
the concert home, and one day the piano stood dead.

I walked to her door to see her husband.
The lady that helped me see my tune, is now playing her own.
The piano stood dead, among the music notes that held her soul.

Her teachings are as if her voice was forte.
My fears were subsequently resounded by heartbeats in pianissimo.
She gave me tears and a new tempo in her breath

I remember the music, the soul
Blazing my own, the keys of life go farther than the piano
The piano stood dead.
I, the piano, and all her students will remember
the whimsical home that found a chord
within our voiceless
voidless lives.

Soil Plus Water

All of you took many blows, heartbreaks, and struggles.
L.A is a city unlike any other; it's cold, desolate, but thrives within the inner.
You see the eloteros and you see hope; you see the honest worker and he gets respect; you understand the man on the porch, the women praying at her statue of Jesus,
the cries of the tamale lady outside your door. Give yourself a reminder.
This is key and with it hope: a reminder you are not that easy to be taken apart
and many of your friends were lost,
bloodied in a cross, baptised by faith, blessed with inequities,
held by hellish sights, freed by God's grace, burned by righteousness.
Can you still move on? Cleansed by angels, two wings with bullets around the neck.
Do you still have faith? Ghetto angels are your blessings.
God bless the living; South Central revives the dead.
Golden opportunities to be unacknowledged
Hear my sermon; feel the passion because of their joy.
Let their lost passion become your energy.
They will be a requiem for your living. We have dreams!!!
Don't deprive them of the soul and utmost talent.
If it rains and you're building ground,
start your foundation from there,
and when you climb
over all the blows, heartbreaks, and struggles,
remember you climbed out the mud.

The Area I Hold Dear

I was born in Delaware
moved to Arizona
studied in Fresno
matured in LA
but when I entered LA, I was just a boy

Unknowing of the divisions
unknowking of the hopes, the dreams, of those wanting to make it out
I made them my battle scars
my stories, my emblem, my symbol, my pride, my courage, my strength,
my struggle.

To be a black man from South Central is like a target on your back, but for me it's a symbol of pride
I grew up in South Central, my faith sprouted in ministry.
My dreams used football to nurture my inner ministry
My body enduring pain, generational trauma, inner city discrepancies, the back of the bus during football games was my place of peace besides the doors of classrooms bombarded with old textbooks but teachers willing to make a future for those many gave up on.

Call it battles,
I call it war
Each time I get a victory,
I look at the Morgan Boy
I once dreamed of times like this.

PART 1

Smaller Moves

You are big in oppression
Quiet down
Quiet down
Fan the fires to douse out generational fear
Clasp the back of my hand blessed with ahimsa
Lead the prayer, lead the marches
Confess your fears, your thoughts, we feel your honest intention
Now bring to me your crocodile tears
Or the fire that sears
The generational wounds that are reopening again
You can listen, you can cry, be angry, laugh
But I will never pray for my own downfall
My skin is an eternal marathon
That will outlast the marches
I will be protesting my entire life
Thousands were arrested to bring down four
You spoke of truth after another already fought it four years ago
It's popular to be in the right when it's a social movement right?
Numbers talk, your actions stalk
The corner of a movement that long should be heard
But we must continue to fight for better days
To burn bridges of hate
To operate under systematic seams of woven impressions on a different level
Small moves, big moves
You're moving, moving forward
Turn that into action: we got to keep painting the other side of the fence.

We Take Precaution

Black freedom, black anger, black nonviolence
Then replace those with colors that are privileged
Replace those with stolen artifacts decorated in museums
Replace that with language of oppressors
Replace that with officers abiding to protect and those who aim to kill
All established within an institutional rooted system burned to destroy black expression
With my hands on the ground, I lay peace
With my neck on the ground, I say rest
With my oxygen amounting to trash splattered on the ground, I say I can't breathe
Yet we take precaution, I'm raising my hands in prayer
To a creator and to cry out injustice
Abiding my time keeping sane in an environment where my skin is tagged with a metaphysical order to kill and be suppressed
Ancestors I hear you, black and brown people I feel your fire and desire for peace
The outcome can be changed
Items can be replaced and rearranged
A celly is a tool, a lifeline, a precaution
This is America
This is America
We must take precaution.

Be Fruitful

The expression of the oppression pressed against our skins cannot be dealt with promises that bear no fruit.

Temporary bandages can't heal the upheaval of generational reforms.

Solid solutions must be cemented through consistent directed effort.

Do we rise from uncertainty? Do we live for the promise, the time, the now?

Why wait? The time is here, the action is clear.

We need our accountability, power, voice, control, and freedom.

Imagine what can arise when we overturn systematic roots? Free those who were wronged, prosecute those who murdered our fellow people in their sleep.

Time will tell. For now I'm tired of witnessing unripe fruit with dangled promises, freed killers, and the murder of innocent marganilized people. I'm tired of sipping tea.

Wild Thoughts

I hear my blood
singing a tune as my heart
beats with the smell of deep red crimson.
I see what that sound from my arteries' hemoglobin levels are doing,
a quartet of pain stretching from the immediate temples of my core vessels
down to the streams of barren vessels that lie in my chambers, anemia
stricken, and symbolic cries
from the inside of my achy pitch black heart. It is a machine
with a hue of a sounding cymbal
crashing down on my organs, sympathizing with the rest of my body.
Chest pains accompany only heartbreaks,
a sight only known as a scarlet memory to one's self image
that encompasses fire. It is the wheezing of the left side of my chest,
it screams red. I see a pool of blue symphony
in the middle of my mind. I am wildly racing through my heart,
go-carts on overdrive racing cherry-red
and brick red materials to my heart. They crash across the cardinal
door that is the beat of my cardinal rose aorta wall,
1 millimeter thick all around, encircling my chest like a rusty flaming
cage.
The music plays, the blood is singing with a taste of cherry
flavored gum, mourning ruby tears over the loss of play
and the beating violet red piano plays another tune: it's an encore.

Let's Play Contain the Heart!!!

I have kept (almost) all your commandments.
I have been a great help to your endless mission,
but this heart I carry is darkened with fear. You can't see inside it;
it is an empty toy container, reflective of empty promises,
yet I have been in your support group since I was just a boy!
Now, what will you do when I'm gone?
1, 2, 3, 4, no 5 times I have almost left your side playing this game,
staying within this challenge you call life,
yet working with a playful destructive heart called death.
You have cut my life to a commercial,
cut me away from your angelic route.

My body is a canceled game show.
Let's play along to your commandments. I accept the challenge.
I created all that I can with nothing that I own.
You supplied pieces that aided but also tricked me,
fooling me to the point that I had a need for reminders of my conditions.
I thought there were bonus prizes, a chance to change my mistakes.
My soul is an empty prize box, fill me with your presence

You won't be able to fulfill me when I die,
so why burden me with these chutes and ladders, scrabbles in language?
My body is like Operation but there are too many pieces of my heart to pick up.
Quit pretending to fulfill my dream, I don't want false game pieces mixing with my organs.
No more overtime promises, bland human commitments, no false wildcard prophets. Answer
the question on your life before I breathe the final breath.

Faces

Our brothers and sisters are hanging
on trees like fruit picked ripe from racial hatred and strife.
A week goes by and black men pour out blessings to their ancestors;
so many times a leader stands and it is out of ignorance that we wait until they bleed,
then we react, to heed the message
then we struggle to repel the guilt of what we should've been doing in the first place.
Repeat with messages crossing with social media and action.
Repeat with signs that are directed at infrastructures that hold dead weight.
Police the police until they don't want to be treated with our treatment:
hopelessness, oppressed by higher powers, staggered
wanting to go back to our loving families
unharmed, with stories of love
not lying in streets
not lying in parking lots
not lying in our homes
not lying in the parks
dead, dead, dead, dead: we are displaying the same message.
It's been a 400 year cycle.

Pressure Within My Rainforest

Who would deserve a place in my rainforest
where leaves are broken buildings?
The rain pours smoke and gas from generation to generation.
The locals that were teemed with life are now moved away for boba stores
that are quickly assembled amongst old roots.
Ask yourself this question, "Do I deserve a trip out the jungle?"
Going the spaces which where the essence of a culture dying and then recycling
like the clouds that effortlessly vacate your mind.
I'm betting not, I held a disdain look in their place; I hold myself and my laughter
cry
I sit back, I sit up, and wonder in this jungle
wondering how these new additions leave me out of your social nightmare.
Listening to the sound of my voice as a statistic,
should I roar authority as a man or a beast
and will there be a difference in the force used?
Will I be displayed in front of others in this concrete jungle?
A story posted whenever I venture out or donate my thoughts as contributions to urban society and that grand scheme of equal standard living for all.
The serene grace of it all renders you. This is my living project: to live. To not live fully is death.
Whenever I see people try to escape this jungle and be aware,
I see people walking into my jungle blind.

Soap

Life slipped from my hands like dove soap.
Soft, smooth and sweet-smelling fragrance whispers to me.
It never leaves the bathroom, my space of peace, of cleanliness.
But it is always hard to hold a firm grip on both the smell and the soap.
Only when the bar is not tested with the torrents in the shower can I hold it.
I rub off the life that is within its powder-white as it envelops me with joy.

To clean, to purify, to love, I want to embrace it all around me.
It is all well and wonderful until it opens my eyes, the soap attacks my sight.
Pain stings my surroundings, the suds shut my vision of what's near me.
It stings and stings some more, I cry wanting to take some of the attacking soap away
I poured water into my eyes, I didn't want to see that part of life anymore.
That sweet-smelling pain masked parts of the soap that were long eroded before its use.

I loved the smell but hated the embrace, especially when I see it for what it is.
I always masked it with the smell but the pain it brings cannot be concealed.
Of course, it cleaned me up but overall I was cleaning the body soap.
I was the one giving it purpose, without my body it loses purpose.
It is my bar of dove soap, and no one else's.
I try to clean again and it falls down the drain.

**Wanda Coleman,
the Great Poet and
Unofficial Laureate of
Los Angeles (1946-2013)
Right This Minute! (Inspired by
Wanda Coleman's poem
PERHAPS BY THEN)**

Perhaps by then in the crowded museum, the dark cinema house would empty itself with bliss.
Let's turn the camera on and reflect, edging closer to the fire where our passions burn to a place where our lives are full of incomprehensible deeds and acts.
Maybe we can add to the paintings that stain and sting the eyes with furniture that do the same. The contacts or glasses from long exposure only lifts that dimly lit room. With a seldom telephone, the heat in the air to be home in an ocean casted by a sea of incense. We hear sweet jazz music, with the fireworks outside our door constantly swirling at the time where the moon pushes over the sun.
Our bare hands that have a need for constant noon day run production and prefer empty houses and robust workplaces. The days that we sat dreaming, grasping at multiple stars instead of straws on who will pay the bills. We will find ourselves with the rhythms we call our poetry, our disregarded history in the bodies that do not care and at the drop of a dime, clasp their affection to the screen of good deeds as if a movie is rolling
…perhaps now.

I'll Give You Raw Roses: A Resonating Message
After Artist Rosatzin

The colonial name of Artist Rosatzin was too aggressive, so they sought the ancestors of their painting of what the Nahuatl word Cihuatzin," plural for womxn, meant and combined it with their name Rosa. From brother ce Tochtli and his gathering of knowledge, the tzin is a suffix for honor and respect.

My raw roses are from my Yollotl, which means heart in Nahuatl
and as most of my experiences were formed from people harming my flowers
with gender based violence and the deflowering of my ancestors roots,
I look towards my art, my garden of soulful connections.
As I look at the murals of South Central LA,
I see the street vendors, the small biz, yet also the insensitivity. I am told that I am too sensitive
with men and their women defending them, all trying to desecrate my garden.
They won't stagnate my roots with their opinions.
There are artists and there are people with skill. I noticed artists are generally more sensitive and that's not necessarily a bad thing. It's about what they plant.
Because of this sensitivity artists can envision life beyond the logical and mechanical.
I look towards my intuition, my strength as a womxn growing into a more non-binary identity that sensitivity is even more problematic, that they try to contain me in boxes that never fit my roots
Why do you think roses are sensitive? They need thorns as protection

I don't coddle patriarchy, nor the men that crave to be painted. I paint femme, women, or neutral figures to give a gaze that makes people look away from the misogynistic male gaze.
Very few have access to my petals and that's how it's going to be no matter the timeline.
I will empower my body and my self esteem and channel the painting of colorful bodies and impact more womxn to paint, to create, to break the weed that is patriarchy.

As I paint and create, I also have learned to recognize my needs. An outlet of my emotions and art is needed, I need full circle expression in this garden.

My art is a performance within the little theatre I call a room I learned through art to nurture it and hold space and purge any unhealthy sensitivity healthily.

I've grown up with womxn of various shapes so I am sensitive to that too. I urge those to continue to give people their raw roses, their unearthed rose treasures.

For those doubting my art, I really have nothing to say. They are already entertaining their doubts of me and my work. They serve as compost for my next beautiful masterpiece.

Cold World High

The cold world is the place where illusions of icicles pay my taxes

where the coldness of heart is encased with greed
freezing the standards of those who once had morals.
The cold world is a standard of greed, to feed more cold souls.
The more money you gain, the more your heart loses a chance to thaw.

The cold air attacks my bloodstream corrupted with cash flow, rapidly
speeding my heart towards inflation
tearing through my system and ripping apart families.

The hood is cold, a street conquered by cold people
who froze their own hearts overtime.

My ideas are not cold for without the shock of frostbite,
I would not feel the boiling desire to help my community.

My brain freezes,
my heart warms away
from the sub-zero high that is greed
South Central is not an ice tray for gentrification.

All In

They paint us with broken oppression
easels on easels of black portraits with red lines through their soul. I ask you all today:
How can you give a portrayal of the black experience when you can barely see your own ignorance?
We are all in when we need soldiers, entertainment, culture, and social media.
I am the grandson of a Black Panther, the son to a parent that served their country.
At 16 I preached my trial sermon, at 18 I became a minister, at 21 a seasonal football chaplain. I am all into the fears of not coming home, to see my people in fear and also anger at what police are doing to our fellow blacks on the streets and surprisingly in their own homes.

They painted my ancestors as clowns, but who ran the circus?
Who turned their eyes to us when they needed to fight for freedom centuries ago?
How can all lives matter when we were considered three-fifths?
We are asked to be compliant, to live not less than a century freed from the term
slave, only to be colonized into having 400 years of enslavement on us.
Now I ask all the people gathered today to protest:
Are we tired of not being given permission to breathe in your custody?
To have forces aimed at our heads to destroy us?

To have them paint us in positions of cowardice only to hide their fear of change, of
reform. To be seen as the violent ones, the ones destined to be enchained by another's desire,
something that hasn't been received in over 400 years: to be free within an institution that tries to enslave us.
They took a black man down and had the gall to say all lives matter.
I protest everyday because my skin is a part of the rebellion.

Hood Pie

Crack open a sauntering beetle within a bowl of milk and cereal crumbs.
Open a plate of food stamps and dump its value in the bowl.
After that sprinkle a light work of salty oppression and hefty colonialism.
Leave in the half shoddy oven for 15 minutes.

Take it out of the oven, scorch it, then say a limitless prayer about its crust.
and batter the pie with the Statue of Liberty over and over again.
Do that until the pie tastes like the mixed emotions one has for kneeling during the national anthem, raising a black power fist, or seasoning a new generation with productive ideologies.
Attack the murky conclusions of race and social class.
Cut open the supposedly broken body cams of loping officers strung along the sidewalk.
Piece apart their guns and simmer the pie for more than a minute.

Stir and say I can't breathe.

Proceed to flatten the pie with more lethal force.
Flatten gently as only darker pies get this treatment,
Remove the impurities from lighter pies.
but with darker pies, they need more color.

Continue to disparage the pie until it begins to want to change its color on its own.
Gauge the level of rising injustice in the pie.
If it is ripe, then release it with another Jim Crow act that separates the pie in quarters.
When it is almost done, divide it more so that they can never be all on the same side.

Place fake trimmings and chains along the sides of the pie
Adorn the pie with false convictions, media disapproval, and social inequities;
that's how you obtain the infamous hood pie.
    Hesitantly more pies are popping up in the shops of South Central all for the great cause, right?

Sumn' Like Black Panther
(Inspired by the Marvel Movie and Kendrick's Lamar's album "Black Panther")

My grandma was a Black Panther, a leader for her people.
New York was her city, her jungle.
Underneath the spiritual, the physical, and the mental, I was a panther too.
Where did my fangs go? My prowl?

Were my studies a product of the stomping grounds I paved?
Is this the experience that my forefathers wished for when they were enslaved?
Where are the commas, the compliments given between pity?
I represent a street in Morgan, all in the infamous part of a city.

But my grandma sees it too, the acts that will outlast me.
The energy I give is the same, I want to go past me.

My kingdom in LA, all an illusion to gentrifying outsiders, unknown, built in stacks.
Pressed in black panthers DNA, modern day combat mode deactivated mixed mental attacks.

Black and black and extras that I say: king, your strength is building.
King, rise above the love, open the doors that have been shutoff from receiving indigenous healing

King of my city, king of hungry, king of my fate as if it's Wakanda's homestand,
king of the filthy, I called the trash out; king of the culture, they wanted to cash out; king of empathy, everyone can be spoken on skyscrapers.
I dodged haters and I got on their heads like fresh tapers.
I never built my kingdom like a fool because I can see through your tricks.
You tried to punch through my soul, but either way I end up with kicks, custom made, custom of the fade, I run fade, I am made.
Black Panther calling my name, Grandma started the game
with my brother's tat, my endless spat.
That the bloodline never was the same, when we ran with Black Panthers.

Goodbye To Normal Days

My emotions are obsidian birds paved with long-lived mobillity
as my feelings seep in darkness, they caw at dredged ceilings
or at the bloody ringing, the bell that signals my feelings
to fly around, with a purpose to find a warming endearing home
to look for unwelcoming monochrome heartbeats and troubles.

Fleeting and surfing with waves of blue and white scarring
the sky. Yet with the pollution, the helicopters like crows taking
any chances of freedom away, how can I fly?
When will we be free of the constant crows? The policies that hold
my wings in place seemingly edit the sky until it decays.
All while the cage of gentrification draws ever near;
there's no mistake. My emotions take off and here I am in flight.
Flying, with wings dry of age and tragedy,
yet I'm wide awake to fill the burdens casually seen like a
washed tormented angel with lost wings, undaunted by change.

Yet no matter the challenge, I will gain wings in that cage.
You will see me fly beyond what tries to limit me.
I will not be stranded mid-flight between fear nor lack the
sunshine on my travels, for which my heart holds ever dear
I still fly, with nowhere to depart to in this dark glitching sky
to wait upon the darkness and sit with evil passing by.
I am a lark, an obsidian bird committed to eternal flight
---in endless freefall with my heart in a cage.

Your Own Heroic Survival

You are the apocalyptic survivor from the war of losses
walking along with human nature
burning, innocent, writhing in pain from the loss in life
but you keep going
propelled like anger-filled warnings across the humid air
littered among the remains of dreaded wishes and wants tied to cheap
threads. Only until you heed my warnings but then it is too late as
you have noticed your emotions were poorly cut from stone agendas within a deep cloth of great mistrust.
You have barricaded yourself within illusions you cannot defeat.

Where is the cape that you adorn with medals,
the medallions you shaped out of broken mirrors?
I thought you said you embrace poverty?
I thought the hood made you a killa?
So when did being a hero make you a leader?

I will tell you this my hapless friend,
you are shut within your own shelter of emotions.
I refuse such a simplistic living.
I will choose love over sad faces,
faces mared, jarred with villainous glass shards of cordless happiness, I
hold no comfort for those willing to place people back.

If no one will save me from myself,
then I will work towards my pain and tell others that sadly
my world, a world with a sanity of shaded pain,
can never be possible unless those are willing to open
and cut down misunderstanding
and choose trust and inner love instead.
When survival is the only meal you had,
where would the lie be in sheltering your own fears?

My Eyes Were On Philadelphia
*This poem focuses on Philadelphia street in Whittier, California.

Amber buses,
floating Fed-ex autos moving
making pleasure into padlocked traffic
singing Philadelphia, the home of the Brave,
the street of the fallen Honda,
the smiling Tesla, unable to falter economic deep water; breakfast is moving like hotcakes.
People love to eat up their space and time like dust.
Moving is a homeless mission: brown, blue, green butterflies of mirages.
Greens ever with life and death, ideals of watchful people
leaves will never leave above the economic,
the streets will be filled and closed to the needy,
broken buildings, broken before we moved in;
parking never housed any hearts but people keep working,
appropriating their ideals of living life.

The people on the bottom as the poor sit on the benches
and the benches sitting strife.
The parking, barking, astounding and the cheers
and the cadavers of the naggers are always clear.
Available, the complaints;
unavailable, the solutions to house a being.

Giveth and giveth ideas but never agreeing
This brotherly road cutting ever deep into the ample traffic
My humble abode, and my eyes were on Philadelphia.

PART 2

And You Hated Me

And you broke me, a man among tendrils of red houses.
These lousy mixed martial arts feelings, tampered by spouses
riddled with lies and beyond hopes.
I know you enjoy the pain
that my chocolate M & M skin endures
being on the side of lies with eyes as anonymous as left Tinder swipes.
Who can you tell my story to?
The woman beside a cheating husband who brings ragged deals to South Central,
the man who is not at all marveled
by his bitter, heavy hitter slugger that is his beautiful
darling's starry enlarging fist that gets closer to his face. And then it hits him; then he begins to hear what he was missing.
Unable to hear the children crying, unable to hear the children outside
along the strands of a family home
crying for milk haplessly mixed with 40 ounces. Crawling under shards of Hennessy bottles relentlessly engaging the amber trash with the pursuit of cop cars to be put to sleep.
Playing tag in the sky with helicopters searching for suspects.
Ropes, tied my neck like the criminal justice system.
A tendril of red houses and blue houses mixed with purple indecision.
I decided to frame you as my hero. Now I am the slugger. I am the mixed martial artist. I earned my black belt by being belted by police patrolmen all while taking routes to avoid the enforcers of the streets and laws.
Along the bitter magic called weed and henny
affiliated with these minions,
I began to recuse myself into nothing

South Central Dreamer: A Narrative Inspired By A Jefferson HS Alumni

Until high school, I didn't realize how important it was to have citizenship
In the 9th grade, the University of Southern California was a guest for my AVID class.
It was an Upward Bound Program which allowed high school students to earn college credit while in high school, a way out to freedom and educational opportunities.
I had no social security, and my tears migrated like butterflies.
My teachers encouraged me, told me that college was near my gaze.
They fed me with an air of positive thoughts, that braved through a world of no job.
I dreamed of a world where I could support my family
A world outside South Central where I could spread my wings
and nest and grow in a struggle many never knew.
I wanted to fly gracefully, and when Deferred Action for Childhood Arrivals (DACA) was passed in 2012, I was very delighted to hear the news.

Yet $495 stopped my wings; I dared not to ask my mother, a single mom taking care of three kids, to add another burden on her heavy wings. That same year I was a member of a non- profit organization called A Place Called Home.
It was my place and I called it home, and through it I worked as an administrative assistant for the organization, learned a lot of skills, and got closer to a work permit.
Then I finally opened my wings, I applied for DACA and received a social security card, a work permit, and a California ID.
I flew high with opportunities like the internship with Metropolitan Water District of Southern California and I have traveled to Sacramento, California.
In high school, I ran the marathon and was valedictorian. Soon I will be able to rest amongst the comforts of a new home that I own.

I am happy that the superior court decided to stop Trump from ending it.
He won't stop our migration, he will not stop my flight. I am a dreamer, a South Central dreamer.
Through uncertainty, I hope and pray that the Senate passes the bill called

American Dream and Promise Act. The Democrats in the House of Representatives passed the bill; the Senate has to continue the dream.
No matter the danger, no matter the challenge, I will rise like a monarch butterfly and migrate to make a difference in the world whose wings are severed; my flight will carry the dreams of many. I now know the importance of having citizenship; I fly my dreams around South Central.

LLD (Our Dreams Have Angels): Rest In Peace Davon "Rico" Spillers

"I'm never gonna die, never heard of death, energy can never be destroyed only the flesh"
-Nas

Sorrow tumbled, tears rolled down my face. But I know he's in a higher place.
I set my blessings to the sky and I said to my fallen friend, "why?"
I place my heart over that chip, I place my start on that trip
I never saw the tormented souls around me as a sanctuary to dwell.
My grief arose in isolation and it's closing walls contained evils to dispel.
That the 5 dollars I left him in his bag during a basketball game, to him was so close and dear
He told me his appreciation like a rainfall and made his sincerity loud and clear
When his time on earth left, I made raindrops seem like showers
I held my voice, while I cried inside for hours.
I placed my hands above the sky to hear a prayer;
I wanted God to provide his soul with reasonable care.
I give them rest as ghetto angels, eastside combatants, war babies, ideals that are settled to be redeemed.
Their narratives rest with the living, and their willingness to be undreamed.
Who pressed their wings to the ground to be engraved?
Who led my now guardian angel to this early hope, not paved?
The marathon continues and no weapon shall overrule, the wounded tears running down on my face.
The tears we shed are a motivation to reset our minds and fuel
the ones who rest in peace with intentional mercy and grace.
Love yourself.

Commandments of Ross Snyder Park

Thou shall not leave your riches behind.
Thou shall not erase graffiti or pick up bags of cocaine you find.
Thou shall not sign gang signs on hands with solid color shirts.
Thou shall not leave blunts outside on the slide, as it brings up a curse.
And thou shall leave children in the park smoking weed alone
Even when you see your son or daughter smoking in the street.
When the police call you and say that the park is an unsafe combat zone,
Thou shall remind yourself the dealer at the park has your ends meet.
Thou shall only call 9-1-1 on a burner phone.
When you walk into the park, thou shall pay respect to your elders.
And when you hear guns run amok, thou shall ruin fences built by welders
As the fences will be fixed but scars will be left on the body and stain.
Your body will lie on the park soil, the blood won't be washed by rain
Thou shall not drink the bitter waters or go to the park at night.
Thou shall hang with the gang members, unless you want a fade on sight.
These are the commandments of Ross, the park of Morgan, my home.
Follow these to preserve organs, duck your heavy head when you hear
gunshots or see chrome.

I Fought Divide

El Salvadorians
and Mexicans clash in the crowded school-yard green.
I cannot remember the bodies
just blood
splattered among
blades of fresh grass like dropped sweet Jamaica
among clothes, uniforms wrapped in
unheard punches

and lunches
spewn from the mouths of pained Mexican boys
and girls, from brown punches
teeth shatter
and blacks,
siding with their respective gangs. Their rugged attitudes
bloodied across borders, losing hope,
families torn.

Without hope,
holding battles on their own bruised backs, faces
to beat up their enemies
by race
and nationality
with prideful ruined nations on scorned youthful backs.
Mexicans beating in allEl-Salvadorian
bodies relentlessly

all while
security guards pulled them away, with blacks seeing
horrendous actions, demonstrating street cred
and brutality
give me,
my arms and restrain my friends beating himself
over his head for not
respecting heritage

Slauson Elegy: Homage to the Martyr of South Central

Nipsey Hussle ran a marathon. I was a spectator. He served his street, his community. I saw him hold bandaged homeless soldiers from the results of conflicts in their hoods.

He was the only soldier in a ragtag group of South Central cadets, last time I checked. Reconnecting his community brought gangs together who were torn at red and blue strings among the Slauson soul food restaurants, he was their King of Soul, but the toll was whole.
And the flashes of wonder, the thunder that Nipsey came to be on metro buses to parks.

When I was bitter enough to see, the whole community had to wipe their eyes and say RIP.

To his final race, a chase I couldn't dare, or didn't care because I didn't want bullets near.

The sign of the people crying, the shooter's family dying, and graffiti on streets with "TMC," the babies following their mother's grief, the mothers following their husbands and lovers' beliefs, his homeboys in disbelief, with belief that he hadn't done enough yet, no not yet Nip,
he shouldn't have been casted out the earth. God why do the legends die so early?

His marathon shouldn't have ended, the baton should not be passed with ghastly prayers. His sons aren't men yet, they get the baton to fight battles up steep hills, and cheap thrills.
The mothers of his children carry the baton, his spirit, with guidance and love.

Nipsey told me these streets weren't for you, so I dare not venture out my place.

Where the henny and hash don't pass me up on the bitter steps to hell where the burning desires of nighttime cheers, of morning blue and night red mixed with the corpses of innocent children.

For the blood had cycled in reps in Slauson, from the rows of unsettling greed, that ended Nip and it cycled back to the streets, repeating the struggle and the vicious lie that redeems.

The areas remorse, and find the source of the angry drummers kneeling and playing vicious beats upon the drums that Nipsey gave to them from his album.

The choir used their spirited souls to uplift the parted souls of Ermias to their ideal of heaven. And we wonder where the Slauson spirit goes, where is it's next hero, the next fate for a legend. We wait for guidance upon the trivial nonsense we call human life, death,

but we give homage to the hero that made an unwanted name to a brand, to a street.
He made a marathon that will continue to stretch above the earth and the heavens.
The baton is placed, the markers are set, and it's time to break records, all as an elegy for Nipsey.

Dealer of Hooper Avenue

As he places the blunts towards the flame
Upon the silver tray that holds the ash
The ashes within, the holding of sin, a name
Only held with the henny and hash

His beard is scruffy, clothes are ruffy
With his dreads bouncing off the ground
And as he packs his drugs into his duffy
Hooper hears his malicious, vicious sound

"Come one, come all to the end of the street, the strong and the meek
Where I can sell you drugs, henny, and other desires you seek"

And as I place my hopes on the fated faded east side
Of black babies, maybes, and lies
You could never tell that that dealer cried
When he saw 7 year old children using his supplies.

The Standing Memories of A Watt's Native

There have been so many years that come back repeating themselves even with one look back there come three separate statements with an amazing purpose. A list of reminders and flashbacks never make a visit without their being a creation of partners along. The distance is thought with the thousand pieces that are warmly and quietly waiting to be framed and admired. So many years come back and the reason why it came is not for the reminder, but for the vision that it gives, the same reason it left safely is the same way the visit becomes after its thought. Whenever genuine thought is knocking on the door, that's when everything else shuts off, and my mind is stuck on why the role is even happening. The exploration of each memory is all, aside from the blank space that exists with the afterthought. Why has it been waiting to be found and dug in to understand the reason why it was even allowed to be thrown away for some time. Memories that bring back an explanation that just brings everyone back together.

The best one is probably realizing where you come from and understanding the meaning it truly shares. Remembering that I wasn't able to play with the older kids because there were so many restrictions. The ones that as soon as I took a step forward would give me a lap backward, as they would say. It was like every move mattered, but having all my moves to be locked behind a black gate that I can only look outside to know what it is that's really happening. You would need an arm to fully grasp you to fully understand the full concept. To leap back is to leap forward and yet every whisper holds you down. Every whisper that was heard is what really mattered as soon as the word went out because there's really no way out and behind the gate is where all this started. All the echoes to each other because sometimes we needed both the arms to shoot the echoes in order to keep the real silence. All these clues that were given, but not many found the real one, just the full excitement and the full pin drops.

Standing behind the black gates just made everyone blind-sighted with the memory, not here there wasn't much to look at if it wasn't the birds in the morning humming to all the neighbor's music while they swept their front porches. The type of gates that go on forever that don't reach the end until the trash is laid out. The ones that never oppose what is ready to be set for the neighbors next generation that hold more than the memory that never goes away because it's always told. The stronghold of the way it stands is what everyone looks at as we pass on through the regular streets that are waiting to be memorized again.

The Light in the Classroom

As I looked into the classroom, there was so much light and many lessons. Everyday he posted a quote, a message that will lead us to a better future, from the creation of the world, to the heroes, to his own life lessons.

From the jeers of his students, the disgruntledness of others not understanding
and playing his words as if they were nonsense,
I was one that listened and understood the depth of his teachings.

One of my close friends, Byron, knew, sitting right next to him that these teachings would impact us.
We endured taunting for some didn't understand what it meant to have a leader such as him.
We looked forward to the next day, the English tests, the work he carefully selected to make his students think.
We always had our hands up eager to push ourselves and our classmates forward. When we fell short, we rose again.

From the learning of new vocabulary, to book reports, and his want for his students to rise and do better than the environment we have around us.

The books are decades old, the books scribbled and reused, and the use of materials dwindled. I look back at his teachings and where his approach to literature opened my writing. He gave me hope, his direction was clear amidst the violence and the infrastructure around us that teemed with potential.

His sternness, his quick and fair judgement, and understanding propelled me to love literature more. From his lessons my own wisdom grew.

We read *Gilgamesh*, *The Iliad*, and *The Odyssey*. We were close with our direction and his knowledge helped us to prepare for the next steps.

To quote Byron he states that " I'd really liked this time where we were truly learning what it meant to learn to think," and I couldn't agree with him more.

The activities Mr. Martinez-Cruz gave us were made into life lessons that have been carried in my academics 'til this day.

As I look back now, as a 2nd year Masters of Divinity student at Yale Divinity School that was accepted to over 6 grad schools, awarded the Most Outstanding Contribution to the Religious Studies Department by my professors at Whittier College, and now pursuing my dreams,
I look back at the teacher that believed in me, the one who first put light in the classroom.

One Shot Will Heal You

I am on another level, one test away from kindness
I have a shattered view of the distant world
Nothing works my way for good reason
Whose lucks shoots them across stars, without leaving fragments behind
Order is needed, greed does not play a role

Why can't we all be equal?
What's the cost of freedom?
My medicine is like bullets
I can't feel enough
I can't heal enough

Send my body across the shores of liberty
And then reject my people with codes and standards
The law that you have does permit me to grind and move forward
The medicine hurts more than the injury itself

Healing is damaging to me
That is my witness, my listless way of solving my own problems
I cannot change unless I repeat the steps that made me grow
Alas glass castles will fall, mirrors within my warped mentality glisten I
am simply thinking of better days

Across the board I am written to a painful script of recoil.
It hurts as I work to feel the healing
I just can't feel

I can't reload the ammo at times
The doctor said I'm empty on life
My body, the gun, has no more clips

Healthy Homes

Your homes beat South Central to the ground
As your words fiddled on streets
Of broken isles of trash around
I will not be in the room with cheats

As you crawled around my hood
Filling the area with vile filth
And you thought for the good
But it was blood you have spilt

Along lines of fire, that I inquire
The hell for those who've passed
I will not set, nor bet the squire
To whom the magic was cast

And this magic was in fateful domes
Of unroping joys of financial grace
To sell our inner souls and outer homes
And to move to another place

With gentrification deploring my land
And halting fellow members of Vernon
Your greedy cultivating minds take my hand
And make us accept the fate you are earning

Negro Memories Are Available

They have the nerve to call us degenerates but who shipped us to this land?

Liberty, peace and justice are all facades: tell me what happened to Sandra Bland?

Our battles take place in courts, sports and in learning.
We have won some, so have they, but our hearts are still burning.

Black skin isn't an option you're born with; this pigment
Black culture, history and respect is not a prosthetic ligament.

The enemies we face are politicians, yet we got a great shot.
But they hide their racism under a mask and leave the hoods to rot.

I'm glad to be black because I can use my color like a marker.
The 1st man, the 2nd man and the 3rd made history but which one was darker?

They lighten, sully our pride and have the nerve to make us the priced slaves.
We got off of the ships but in our minds, we hopped into graves.

I'm dark as the night and my voice is choppy like you're clapping a syllable.

I put my hand in my jacket and pull out candy or my I.D. that would make me killable.

You have no options available, black is not an optional direction.
Black memories never die, they go through a careful selection.

Heartaches

My heart is a machine
Rebooting and slow to upgrade
caged within scar tissue.
Thick riveting blood paces throughout the arteries;
My breathing is caged. My blood support, my love support does not stem here.
Passion does not either. Veins blue from no oxygen.
Arteries red with sprawling amounts of hemoglobin
These mechanics carry little weight.
The soul does not pierce through this heart
This thick manifestation of blood and tears
I break before my heart does. I pass before my blood is supported with oxygen
Rampant in scarlet
Ravaged by generational curses,
Blessed with a service program in giving
Yet all you see are the cages
All I see are the hearts encaged within bitter bodies.
What heartaches do I need to let free?

Wishful Astronaut

Charles Dickson's "Wishing On A Star"
I see through the book, I see through the future.
Give me how I can help others. A rusty astronaut, a vision of illuminating grace.
May my hopes be given to all, may the sun on my back shine light as my son looks up at me.
Clinging to the answers, my deep impervious wish supports future generations.
My wishes are all upon a star, a greater star than before.
A star made of planets, cosmic energy, and scrap metal.
May these dreams eclipse a connection to the beyond, a telephone line that ascends to the heavens
To call all those before; I wish to call more.
My stagnant stance and raised hands to the starry glory above,
I want to send them back down to this gray earth
And   bestow   it   heavenly   light.

Eastside Be With Me

I talk about it 5 days too late
Hands on my bible, all eyes on my fate
If bullets were burdens, they almost killed my soul
Across the block from Ross Snyder, it all takes it toll
I've been trashed, picked up, and beaten by a landslide
Held two fists in the air, covered in rusted iron so I
could get my hands tied. All my people out here wait
for peace to convene. For helping hands to the homeless,
and riches unseen. When kids look up and down the street,
a police car is what they recognize. 2,000 feet above,
they see police helicopters roaming, all to televize
The hands on the cold war, bloodied by oppression
Eyes on our fall until we are beaten by depression
Rushing, pushing, below waves of systematic body failure and shame
21 years later and I find myself with the same ignant name
South central church boy, Eastside hooligan, LAPD's next victim
No cap and with a cap, both aimed for my head saying who "picked him?"

Resolve Yourself
After Kendrick Lamar

I put my hand in my jacket, full of hopes and dreams ,
a chance to warm the body on that cold dead night
and behind me I saw a cop car flashing past.
My head trembled I looked at myself to feel presentable,
to be apart of society and not any sort that the police would harass my soul
or to hear the beating of a heart already hurt by a system that doesn't care
for its people.

I lifted my head, covered in a bandana with no gang affiliation.
Colors, unlike the gangs in my area, are my daily wear.
As a black man from South Central, I object to how we've been treated!
I thought I had a voice, but we are silenced when alone or
grouped together.

It's full circle, no ceasing, no stop but more chop
and with these cuts from comparing myself to those not marginally
oppressed I know now that I sear through broken bottles of karma.
I see through the darkness of my own heart as a book,
as if I'm taking a page out of The Blacker the Berry, adding to this ethnic
sadness, protected by street code and a pleading family.
Rephrase, grow, and enlighten oneself with praise and action.
This is a requiem for the living.
Some of us are dark as the moon but not a star has shown in the projects.
We caught up on bad habits and they treat our opportunities like useless
objects.

Your unrelenting resolve must be more than the visual picture.

What's In store? A Story of Romeo Doubs

What do you see in the classroom? The football field? What do you see with a canopy of concrete jungles placed along gang markers that only in a gridiron can you find solace?
You look at the times you crafted on that field and made sure you're one of one

When do the cleats match the amount of bread we make?
The times where colors can make us bleed and shatter the realities of low income with the motion of
football pads on to rep a community shattered with intentional lies that it's greater on the other side of promise and compromise on freshly lawned grass holding fading but imminent dreams. Eastside is what I claim, Demos Green and Gold held my name. Jefferson became a place where I place my football accolades, my hopes, my dreams, my older brother that gave everything to put me in pads, to clear away the negativity of the streets

To encourage me to go to Nevada
To encourage me to ball with opportunity
To make my name known in the Mountain West
To gift my fortunes, all I got to the backs of those before me
And the home in South Central that calls my name each time I score victories in the classroom, the football field, and the concrete jungles called gridirons
And when my number is called
Or when my number is counted out
I remember the times I bounced the football on the ground during a live game with no fear, I remember the punt return practices that made me who I am
I see the failures of my losses and the friends I lost who pushed me one step closer
I look at the family that sacrificed all they had to push me in a place to witness greatness The wins, the losses, and those who could never choose which side to turn to
If I played offense or defense, I never wanted to be seen as a special as I worked harder than anyone else
I see that the classroom was my center, the field of balance between my

dreams and maturity and I smile knowing

That one day

I can make a way out for those around me and give a name to my struggle
Not as a breadwinner, the workhorse, the studious scholar, the leader
but as the one who plays the game he loves.

On the Daily: A Reflection Inspired By Jarmaine Doubs

South Central LA has taught me so much from the violence to growing up poor.
I had daily reasons why I wanted to become something bigger than my area.
To shine not as a star but as a beacon for my brother and others like me.
I paid attention daily to my mother and she helped me to become a man of character leading by an example unmatched. Where there was a struggle, she guided me by example, so many examples to appreciate my life and my family.

I am who I am because of South Central. Where people call it a wasteland, I found a goldmine. It's my place; I claim it. I claim the area littered with gang violence, police racism and robbery, a place that robbed me of my character. When I walked, it reminded me of the gang member that verbally abused me and assumed I was gang affiliated. It ties to where an officer racially profiled me and my little brother and assumed we were in gangs. I don't condone it.
My area deserves more, my family needs more, faith needs more.
My hands are clasped both in football and in prayer
When I train these kids, I want to remind them that robbing from vendors is not a part of their culture, nor gangs, nor their generational traumas. They have the power to shift the narrative on things that happen daily in our community.

Football kept me sane and out of trouble, it was a home, the history where on the field I can be something that people would take differently anywhere else: a threat.
Jeff athletics gave me a restoring feeling, a gathering of hope where others are tested or bested everyday.
Coaches like Renny ,Wiltz , Sid , Big Mike, Big T. (may his soul rest in peace), Ed, and Mario helped me grow as a player of not only the game but life as well. These guys specifically always believed and would always tell me to chase my dreams. Wiltz even put me in a position to lead my team all the way to the championship but unfortunately we came up short.
But that's the daily grind, I see it in my brother, my family, the

people I have trained, and my daughter
I do what I need to do on the daily, that's what I placed in my
heart, in my soul, to lead by example and have a better life
To see my brother exceed is one of my biggest hopes and my best
experience at Jeff was witnessing my little brother make history.
He was top 5 in the nation with 44 touchdowns.
I just want to be that daily beacon of light: To relentlessly train my
mind, body, and soul to lead people to a better future here in
South Central on the daily
I want my people to make it out!

Move Buildings, Move People

I cannot land victory with a broken crown
The buildings, like people, are torn down
And they are quickly rebuilt into unstable housing for all my hood to see
Houses without running A/C or cables, and the highest price it'll be

That's a promise on impoverished streets, a contract in the vacant sky
With greasy hands, I pry away all the things that made evil get by
Give me liberty or give me breath
Open to help me get a new home, or reach a lower economic depth

The peace that was once there is gone and the ideal of hope is scattered
Without warning marble pavements and 3 bedroom units are gathered
And sink my standing lower than the masses around
While the city cheers gentrification,
that these murky dark clouds of greed fatally surround

"Alcohol is Law"
(After Kendrick Lamar's "God is a Gangsta")

10 shots down and you wasted, with mental cases
And fill the Holy Grail so blunt priests would get their maces
But if I'm bottled by the danger, no unholy thoughts racing I couldn't run home to my momma no more, my heart's pacing
Everything is so complicated

I open my troubles to peace then my mind turns and frames me as a devil
Was that your ploy, why would my body stoop to your level?
Too many times you lied but only time will tell
You gave me a blessing, then never wished me well
Everything is so complicated

Everything is so complicated when I stopped consuming the bitter drink I left the bottle sitting on my mind,
I left the bottle on the sink
I left the bottle to move forward,
it's a bitter way to cry
I don't want to be in that room no more, the complications hit the sky

Everything is so complicated when each sip makes it worse
If heaven had any laws, no alcohol would be added first
Everything is so complicated

Never Ready

What I got on my mind in Alameda
You strategize, then categorize my feelings
You got everything gone
And you say you wavy
Clean
Pop the grease, hold the gravy
See everything up like it's navy

You never hit the shore, but never mad at you like a bad sweater
But what led you to this twice?
Where did your guap go, where did your cred go?
Reminisce about your old life
And look up on the cold nights
Where you saw your homies with you from the start and then they told you they will finish it for you
Pass the the next baton, clap your hands and flow towards the next element, you are the intelligence
You have the grit, the swag, the culture
But when did you want your momma to not worry about your job?
To be less blind about the dangers around you?

You're going to respect what!?
The West, The East, purple dangers
Where the pain is leaving these streets
And sitting in a classroom
You get the bag and a baffled look on your face
If understanding your muscles creates a paradox of superficial lies and a false creed
Then drop the window, close the curtains, and roll your attention to the sky

Undelivered by the Church

Repressive demonic thoughts peer through judgements.
A minister speaks false prophecy, lies after lies, they say to me.
The jury stands, his day in court is his.
The churchman sits deep into his pulpit
judged by peers, tormented by fears
of his endless disgrace to the church.
How dare he take medication.
Where can you believe this heresy of devil's lettuce?
No treatment unholy will help you, preacher.
He leans and awaits his fate.
Closed now he is from heaven's gate.
But is it owned by the people, or owned by God?
The jury screams guilty, his past friends say filthy,
the minister gives a sad nod.
As the minister speaks his case, he rebuttals to the church this meaning:

You held me close; you held me the most.
Lies you all fabricated before.
This was destined to be, no the church lied to me.
For you went and closed my salvation door
The body is a hypocrite, I know it's hard to admit
That your eyes are bound on conflicted rage,
but when you see my trouble, and all the past rubble,
you would see that it's your heart that is in a cage.
I will get stronger, but my life for not much longer
for my eyes are seeing the end.
If there is a cure, I must know.
If not by good tidings, I'll go.
To meet up in heaven with a friend.

The Sun Rises East

One year, I held it down. I was far too many times the newcomer
a different animal to South Central.
I wasn't the strongest, wasn't the fastest.
It was my mindset. I had a goal to strive to be better,
better than what the hood told me,
better than what my authority held me to,
stronger than the grip teachers tried to place me under.
I knocked all their expectations down with thunder.
You see I picked apart the ghetto to understand my own foundation.
I made my place inhabitable, a safe space. I did my work underneath violence,
did my college applications in the back of the football bus
to show that I was a beast among their standards.

What they could never break was my vitality.
When they expected hospitality, I showed them originality.
          A person making it out of South Central, a man wanting to
better the lives of those in it,
I want to raise Eastside ambassadors, products of the struggle,
futures that will not be erased over race, to be squandered over reputation,
but among the shoulders of an upcoming legend
who just happened to stop by Jefferson High School
home of the demos, among wings green and gold,
with eyes that shone amongst the city lights.

Picket Fences

I'm near a picket fence that contrasts my color and looks to destroy it.
    I am at my wits ends to determine the cause of this rage.
This anger, this hatred from the man behind the gate.
    Does he see me as a person?
    Does he see my race as an eyesore?
What propaganda pushed him to be like this?
    What caused this anger?
Injustice, Injustice, Injustice.
I cry out for an answer for their causes
I question why a fellow man would attack a race and burn the churches.
    Why does a man shoot a church based on hate?
Why would a group persecute fellow human beings?
    Why is war needed?
Why would a man amass these imaginations that minorities are inferior?
Why would a man amass that the people next to him are not in need of love and understanding?
    What gave him this decision, this mission to purge
        to hate, to plunder the liberties of those wanting to live freely?
    What did they do to become like this?
As I sat back on the white picket fence, I took a paintbrush and painted it black.
The man behind the fence went around to hug me.
He said that he didn't see me as a person before.
From the color I placed beyond my own boundary, he saw my narrative.
    Supremacy dies when you know everyone's story.
Ignorance dies when you know everyone's story.
Hatred dies when you know everyone's story.
Color every picket fence.

Acknowledgements

Thank you to my family, friends, and loved ones for helping me become the person I am today. Thank you for helping me achieve a goal farther than what I would have seen.

Thank you, Kevin Weatherbee. You believed in me and with angel wings you are still guiding me. Sunshine, his golden retriever that he brought to class every day, gave me comfort in bettering my stutter. You gave me so much and helped me to see past my color, past what people called a disability, past my anger or my circumstances. You knew when you called me the day I missed the science fair that night, after they said I got first place, that science was my calling. It was from moments like that you amazed me. You were one of the most influential people during my childhood, and my drive to pursue higher education is because of you. When others said to sit, you told me to rise. What else

can I say but thank you? Thank you for helping me be courageous. Mr. Weatherbee inspired so many students to take up their dreams and through this work, I've taken up mine. When you passed away my senior year of high school, giving your eulogy after all the speech training and respect you have given me is one of the most resounding moments of my life. I'll continue to rise, to burn bright with passion, and be the change I want to see in the world. May your soul rest in peace.

South Central Tribute

This is a tribute to a husband, a friend to many, and most importantly a father. He will be missed, his life in South Central is just one of the many voices that are unheard. It is with great honor I give this man a resting place where most would not be: in a book to educate the future. It is to bring light, hope, and most importantly love for the area you rep. This is William Jiles Johnson. This is a tribute to a person from South Central. Rest in peace, power, and love in the arms of the Lord. 7/18/1965 - 7/10/2019

A Moment of Thanks

To Jefferson High School, thank you for the time that I was a Demo. I'll cherish those memories on and on. Thank you Mr. Martinez-Cruz for your guidance, you got me to this point, and I want to say thank you for pushing me. Thank you Demo football (rest in peace, Coach T.) for giving me the mentality to work on my holistic values and for showing me the meaning of family. I know where I'm from: Eastside!!!

Thank you, Davon (Rico). Your life inspired many. You were one of the first friends I met in South Central. I'll keep putting on for the city and the spirit of South Central you valued: This marathon is eternal.
To my one of a kind Big, my dearest friend, Connie Morales, thank you. You inspire me everyday.

Thank you, Orthogonian Society. Do good and do well.

To my pledge brothers, stay timeless owo.
CHHLLNRSTW

To Whittier College, thank you for the ups and downs, my climbs and my falls. It is because of you I have grown to learn, acclimate, train, and acknowledge my sense of holistic care and the body of work I can give to South Central.

To those lost to police brutality, rest in power as well. Rest in peace George Floyd, Eric Garner, Breonna Taylor, Travyon Martin, and all those who have been affected. Your voices will be heard; we hear your cries. We carry on black excellence and the passion to reform; we will be the change.

To my Editors,

Thank you all for reviewing my poetry and placing it to be at the best state it can be!

Jay Green, thank you for your phenomenal work ethic and helping to revise my poetry. Your comments about revising my work and bringing new text to display really helped during the final process of editing. I enjoy the critiques and the work you put forth helping me reach my own goal as well. Continue to be passionate with your work, and one day I would definitely like to collaborate with you on a poetry chapter book of our own. Again, I enjoyed your remarks on my poetry, and they truly helped me to become better both as a creative and as a student in the lifelong craft of poetry.

Ty Lopez, thank you brother for your advice through the mental processing for the book. You have helped me sculpt with placing this book in a way that will not only tell my stories but others in South Central as well. Thank you for all you do bro. Continue to strive in the 4B's and I'm excited with the work you're doing now. Keep grinding, man. Love you pb. Stay timeless.

Professor Tony Barnstone, thank you for reawakening my passion for poetry. It is because of your teachings that I was given this idea to write this memoir. There is more to come. Thank you for reconnecting me with my passion. Continue to inspire generations of creatives.
Elijah, thank you for everything. You really took time with me lol. I wasn't the easiest little brother to deal with but it was because of you I'm where I am now. I can say a lot of things, but I can text and call you with all that lol. This is just the beginning, and I'm proud to write the lineage of Black Panther within us.

Thank you, **Black Minds Publishing** for reviewing and accepting my manuscript, and allowing me to make my dreams into reality. Thank you for taking a chance on *Morgan Boy!!!*

THANK YOU, READER. I HOPE YOU WERE INSPIRED BY MY POETRY.
IT'S FAR FROM OVER, SO STAY TUNED. ALSO CONTINUE TO GRIND AND GROW SPIRITUALLY, MENTALLY, AND PHYSICALLY ON ALL LEVELS.

About the Author

Noah Humphrey (referred to as Knowa Know) was born in Wilmington, Delaware, yet lived in various parts of the West Coast (Yuma, AZ and Fresno, CA) throughout his life until he arrived in his senior year at Thomas Jefferson in South Central, Los Angeles. From his time there, he began to delve into his faith. He preached his trial sermon at 16, became a minister at 18, and earned the title of spiritual advisor and chaplain for the Whittier College football team at 21 years old. Noah earned his bachelors at Whittier College with a major in Religious Studies and minoring in Holistic Care. Currently pursuing his Masters of Divinity at Yale Divinity School, Noah plans to become a professor while entering into chiropractic school with the aim of combining holistic care and neo-spirituality which he believes is key to the life around him. As an Orthogonian, he goes forward and continues to work on himself and empower those around him representing his society's values of leadership and stature. He plans to become a pastor and a chiropractor that utilizes prayer. He spends his time writing poetry, working out, utilizing his free form tai chi, energy healing, bettering his community, and using his artistic talents to help those around him be inspired and develop their own "holistic path."

www.ingramcontent.com/pod-product-compliance
Lightning Source LLC
Chambersburg PA
CBHW071241090426
42736CB00014B/3173